10 SIMPLE STEPS ...

EASY RESEARCH WRITING

A fearless guide to writing perfect research papers

By J.C. Harold

10 Simple Steps... Easy Research Writing

ISBN 978-0-578-41115-6

Published by BDJ Media

DEDICATION

This research writing manual/workbook is dedicated to all my students who have exercised that willing suspension of disbelief by rejecting the quick fix method of writing school papers, choosing instead patience by painstakingly following my outlines, which hopefully have made the writing/research process not only easier but more rewarding!

"A word after a word after a word is power."

—Margaret Atwood

Contents

WRITING THE RESEARCH PAPER

Getting a research paper assignment can be a daunting experience. For this reason, there is a tendency to put it off until the last minute. Bad idea because that's when the project really becomes overwhelming and unmanageable. Why? Think about it. Procrastination is the enemy. Panic sets in, stress levels increase, and what could have been a fun (yes fun!) and challenging assignment becomes the worst experience of your student life. But it doesn't have to be that way. In fact, research papers are probably the easiest academic documents to write. Did I say *easy*? Absolutely! All you have to do is follow a plan. It's like using the GPS on your car: you enter your start and end points and then follow the steps.

That's the easiest and most logical way to approach research paper writing. If you follow the 10 simple steps outlined below, you will also arrive at your destination: a polished and finished research paper! No sweat, no panic, no fear of failure. Moreover, if you religiously follow the simple plan I've outlined for you, most likely you will also ace your assignment!

*

This easy research writing manual is divided into three sections. Please review each one carefully.

Section I outlines each step in the research process, complete with samples for each step.

1

Section II is *your turn* to use the blank worksheets provided for each step to compose your own research paper.

Finally, Section III gives helpful **how-to** hints you will need to compose your paper: how to use a template, which will make your formatting much easier; how to paraphrase, summarize, and quote from your sources—an essential skill when writing your paper; how to compose an abstract.

That's all there is to it! So let's get started!

The Steps

SECTION I – The Steps

Writing the research paper, regardless of the proscribed length, can be broken down into the following steps:

- Identifying your topic (if your instructor has not assigned you a specific topic)

- Narrowing your topic

- Formulating a focus question and research proposal

- Formulating a thesis and establishing research criteria

- Identifying keywords/phrases

- Taking notes

- Composing an outline

- Writing your draft

- Creating in-text citations, cover page, and reference page

- Revising/editing, finalizing, submitting your paper

Whew! That sounds like a lot of work. But it really is not, especially if you follow and complete the easy steps and worksheets in this manual.

Remember, follow each step as outlined. Don't be tempted to skip anything or you will defeat the purpose, just as you would if you ignored the directions on the GPS in your car! What follows is your **Research Paper GPS**. It is designed to get you from your starting point: the blank page, to your destination: the finished research paper.

Happy writing!

Step 1: Identifying your topic

(If your instructor has assigned you a topic, go to Step 2)

Part 1

Before you can begin your research paper, you must have a topic. If your Instructor doesn't assign one to you, you'll have to come up with a topic of your own. Where do you start? It's best to begin with the obvious. What are the subjects that either:

- interest you the most; or

- you would like to know more about?

It's only common sense that if you are already interested in a subject, you will be equally interested in writing about it.

Most of us are interested in a great many things, but for a research paper assignment you have to choose only one topic. The best way to get started is to spend about 5-10 minutes "brainstorming" to create an *interest inventory*.

INTEREST INVENTORY

First select three to five (3-5) general topics that interest you and write them down, leaving enough space between each topic to *brainstorm*. In the sample below, there are five topics of general interest:

- Healthcare

- Employment

- Internet/Social Media

- Climate Change

- Fantasy Literature

Next, consider each general topic and list everything that comes to mind. This is called **brainstorming**. Now look over each list and highlight one item in each list that interested you the most. Take a look at the sample list below:

- Healthcare: future of medicare, opioid addiction, dealing with depression, jobs in medical research, cancer cure, medicine of the future, are GP's obsolete, unfair system, how to change the system, socialized medicine, healthcare for all, should it be mandatory, the responsibility of the health care professional, patients and health care professionals, children of addicts, planned parenthood, elected officials views

- Employment: best jobs for the future, tech industry, unemployment insurance, choosing the right career, US vs. other countries, women make less money than men, the glass ceiling, sexual harassment on the job, is college necessary, energy and new jobs, self-employment, women vs. men in the workplace

- Internet/ Social Media: bullying, teens and social media, dumbing down of America, business and social media, how it affects relationships, dangers, rise of terrorism, fake news websites, how social media influences everyday life, Facebook, lack of privacy, networking

- Climate Change: Future changes in water availability, melting ice and rising sea levels, extinction of animal species (i.e. polar bear), extinction of plant species, difficulty in understanding the facts, global warming: causes and effects, the future of the human race, the future of the planet, is it real, why is it happening, why we can't remain indifferent

- Fantasy Literature: escapism, vampires and werewolves, spells, witches, why are we fascinated by vampires, superhuman characters, Dracula, zombies and cult heroes, the Walking Dead, Game of Thrones, Lord of the Rings, uncharted worlds, living forever, suspending disbelief, emotional high, sexuality and the undead

Part 2

You should now have five (5) items of interest (see highlights above). Next, consider those five items and the pick two (2) that are the most interesting to you. Copy them below (see below).

These are now your ***tentative research topics.***

Tentative research topics:

- Sexual harassment on the job

- Why are we fascinated by vampires

Part 3

Finally, consider the potential of each of your tentative topics by doing a ***preliminary information search*** using at least two (2) of the following:

Consult an online encyclopedia like Encyclopedia Britannica, Scholarpedia (http://www.scholarpedia.org/), or consult http://www.refdesk.com/ for a list of online encyclopedias. Do not use Wikipedia for any of your research. Additionally, you can consult the following:

- A specialized encyclopedia on your topic

- Google, Bing, Lycos, Yahoo, AOL, or a search engine of your choice

- The Virtual Library (`http://www.vlib.org/`)

- Google Scholar

- Infotrac/Proquest

Once you find articles (at least 3) on each tentative topic, briefly skim through the material and decide which one interests you the most and which one has the most information available.

This is now your **RESEARCH PAPER TOPIC** for all the activities that follow. If at any time you find this topic is not working out (e.g., you cannot find enough information on the topic), **STOP** and go back to your interest inventory, select another topic and go through the same steps until you find a topic that you feel is workable.

Once you are satisfied with your topic, proceed to the next step.

Step 2: Narrowing your topic

Narrowing your topic is about going from the general to the specific.

The most difficult part of research writing is probably the step that comes next: **narrowing your topic.** Think of a scene in a TV series you've seen recently where a whole panorama was visible. For example: a scene in *Game of Thrones* where the army of the dead surround a small band of the resistance. Now imagine the camera coming in for a **CLOSE UP** on one soldier, *Jon Snow*, in that scene, and suddenly a multitude of other things are visible to us: distinguishing characteristics like a wound on his face, an expression we could not see before, the fact that there is a scroll sticking out of his amour, and perhaps we can even read some of the words which suggest it is from a loved one waiting for him back home. This transforms our general subject of an army engaged in combat and becomes the story of one soldier, Jon Snow, wondering if this will be his final battle and whether or not he will ever get back to see the loved one who wrote him that letter, and furthermore, wondering where she is at this very moment that his life may hang in the balance. So, what are his thoughts? What is his frame of mind? What we have done is gone from a *general* picture to a *close up* of one man in battle. We have **NARROWED** our subject and gone from the general to some specific aspect.

NOTE: the object of research writing is to learn more about a specific aspect of your topic.

Part 1

Write your topic down on your worksheet. Now make a subheading and title it: **Why I chose this topic.** Then write all the reasons that influenced you to choose this topic (see my sample below).

> **Why I chose this topic:**
>
> Ever since I was a child, I loved to watch movies about vampires and later started reading the vampire novels by Anne Rice, which got me more interested because of the historical roots of the vampire legend and how it traced back all the way to the ancient Egyptians. The fact that a legend could last for so long and finally evolve into the current rages, i.e. The Twilight series, The Vampire Diaries and HBO's campy True Blood is even more intriguing. Why are these creatures so appealing to us, even though they are basically evil and scary – or are they???

Review your list and *highlight* the one aspect of the topic that most interests you (see above).

Part 2

Next, make another subheading: What I already know. Spend 5 minutes jotting down things you already know about your topic. (This can be facts, rumors, statistics, problems, controversies, misconceptions, observations—anything you know already). This information can later be channeled into your own commentary in various sections of the paper, like the **Introduction, Body** and **Conclusion.** See my sample below:

> **What I already know:** Count Dracula wasn't the first "vampire" – actually he was a Romanian warrior whose

name was Vlad the Impaler and he got that name because he impaled the bodies of his enemies on stakes and lined the road to his palace with them as a warning to other potential enemies. But Vlad was actually considered a champion of the Catholic Church and a defender of the faith. Bram Stoker's novel, however, presents a very tormented picture of Count Vlad who basically goes mad after his wife commits suicide and curses God, thereby summoning the powers of hell which grant him immortality. That's one story. Then there are the accounts the account of immortal being in the ancient world, possibly the Pharaohs of Egypt who gained immortality from drinking the blood of their enemies; then there's the story about the plague that swept through Europe in the 14th century. Some people survived by drinking the blood of the infected rats and this gave rise to a change in their DNA, thus creating the first immortals with tainted blood, who became known as vampires. What is most interesting however, is that despite how the vampire legend originated, the vampire himself has gained in popularity, going from a hideous creature to a suave, sophisticated creature of the night with fangs that sucked the blood from willing females who were attracted to him, to today's vampire "hero" who looks like a jock, can stay out in the sun and is a vegan who occasionally sips the blood of animals or human blood procured from blood banks, and does not actually kill people, but is as sexy as ever and women love him.

Part 3

Lastly, make another subheading and title it: **Questions**. Spend 15 minutes brainstorming a list of questions about the topic you've chosen that you'd like to answer in your research. Make the list as long as possible.

> **Questions I would like to answer:** Why are we drawn to vampires? Does it have something to do with our innate desire to live forever? Why are vampires sexy, even when they're killing people? Why are women attracted to them? Are men equally attracted to female vampires? How did the whole vampire legend get started? Was it something historical – an even, maybe, that caused this? If you had a choice, would you become a vampire? Why or why not? Why do other stories get stale and this one never does? What is the essential bottom line appeal here? Why can't we get enough of these blood sucking creatures? Is man naturally drawn to the dark side? The forbidden? Is that why we crave more – just like the vampire craves blood – do we humans crave something we can't have – something so forbidden that we would risk anything to possess it? Is the attraction about having second chances – after all, if you live forever, you can learn from your mistakes and start all over. Do we as humans always want to push the envelope to a new extreme? Do we all have the potential to be vampires? Do we suck the life out of other people – out of ourselves through meaningless jobs or relationships?

After you are finished, look over all your questions and *highlight the one question that interests you the most.* See what I highlighted in my sample above.

14

You are now ready to proceed to the next step.

Step 3: Formulating a focus question and research proposal

Part 1

Go back to the question you highlighted at the end of Step 2 and copy it below. This is your focus question.

Focus Question: Why are we drawn to vampires?

Part 2

Start another file and name it: **Additional Questions**.

Make a list of additional questions (at least five) relating to your focus question that you would like to answer in your research paper. You may draw some of them from your previous list of questions, if suitable. See my sample below.

Additional Questions:

- How did the vampire legend begin?

- What aspects of the legend are most intriguing?

- Why do other stories get stale and this one never does?

- Why are women drawn to these characters?

- Does the vampire fulfill basic human needs and fantasies: the perfect lover, the perfect companion, the perfect protector, the giver of eternal life?

Part 3

Next, decide what **the purpose** will be for your paper. Is it to *explore* your topic, to *argue* your point of view about your topic, or to *analyze* your topic?

- **To explore** – You are posing a question because you are not sure of the answer and wish to discover it in the process of your research.

- **To argue** – You have a very strong conviction or hunch about what the answer to your research question might be, and you want to influence your reader's thinking about it as well.

- **To analyze** – You begin with a theory about your question and then test it by collecting data, and then examining it and determining how closely it conforms to what you originally thought to be true.

The purpose for my paper will be: **to analyze.**

Part 4

Next, you will need to come up with a *claim* or *theory* about your topic. The claim or theory is your position /understanding about your topic and what you will explore, argue or analyze in your paper. How do you come up with a claim/theory about your topic? Simply go over your additional questions list above and highlight the one that you would   like to discuss **in depth** in your paper. The answer to your question will be the **claim** or **theory** you are making about your topic.

Note the question I highlighted on my list of additional questions above. It is now the claim/ theory I will discuss in my paper. Copy that below.

My Claim/Theory: Man is drawn to vampires because the vampire fulfills basic human needs and fantasies.

Part 5

You are ready to formulate your **Research Proposal** using your focus question, your purpose, and your claim/theory. See my sample below:

Research Proposal:

1. **Focus Question:** Why are we drawn to vampires?

2. **Purpose:** to analyze the reasons for this phenomenon based on my:

3. **Claim/theory:** The vampire fulfills basic human needs and fantasies

It's time to begin your preliminary research!

Step 4: Formulating a thesis and establishing research criteria

Developing a research proposal will guide your research process. An effective focus question, purpose, claim/theory has enough depth to help you to develop a **thesis,** which is the main idea that you will discuss in your paper. You may have to revise your thesis statement after you begin your preliminary research.

Part 1

Preliminary Thesis Statement

As you begin the research process, you'll need to draft **a preliminary thesis.** Your thesis is a combination of your topic and your claim which you will then explore, argue or analyze according to 3-5 **criteria** that you establish. The best way to develop a thesis statement and establish criteria is to answer your focus question with 3-5 reasons (criteria), which can be drawn from your claim/theory. See the sample below. I will later use these criteria to find source material.

Topic: Vampires: Our Most Invited Guests

Focus Question: Why are we drawn to vampires?

The answer is my thesis statement as follows:

Thesis statement: It is hardly surprising that mankind has entertained an eternal fascination for the vampire because this mysterious **creature of legend** *(criteria 1)* **appeals to our most basic instincts,** *(criteria 2)* **allows us to engage in fantasy** *(criteria 3)*, and ultimately **rewards us with immortality**, (criteria 4) and all for the price of a simple invitation to let him into our lives.

19

In the body of my research paper, I will use my source material to support this thesis and claim about the vampire according to the four criteria that I have established/highlighted above.

Part 2

Checking for Logical Fallacies

Now before proceeding, try testing the validity of your claim/theory. In order for a claim to be valid, it must be free of *logical fallacies.*

A logical fallacy occurs when one's reasoning is incorrect, which in turn, makes the entire argument invalid. To avoid faulty or incorrect reasoning be sure that you can support your claim/theory with *evidence.* What constitutes evidence? An accumulation of facts, testimony from experts in the field, quotations, statistics, etc., gathered from your research.

Once you begin to compile evidence, avoid making *hasty generalizations*. For example, if you were researching the health benefits of eating strawberries and in your research you found one article stating that three out of six people who consumed strawberries in their breakfast cereal each day developed skin lesions, and you then concluded strawberries should be avoided because they are a health risk, that would be a hasty generalization (based on limited data-- a small study in one article), and thus a logical fallacy.

Closely related to hasty generalizations are *sweeping generalizations*. A sweeping generalization occurs when one applies the results of **one** situation to **all** situations. For example, according to one study, students at University X consume diet cola more than any other beverage offered in the campus vending machines, therefore all college students at all universities prefer to drink diet cola.

You get the idea. So, once you determine that your claim/theory

20

is free of logical fallacies, you are ready to begin looking for sources based on your criteria, which become the **keywords/phrases** you will use in your search.

Step 5: Identifying keywords/phrases

What are keywords/phrases?

Keywords/phrases suggest what your paper is about and serve as important **cues** to guide your research. Usually, they are nouns or noun phrases that you pull directly from the *criteria* you established in your thesis sentence. Often your search will yield greater results if you combine your keywords with your topic. For example, if your research paper topic is about the causes of heart disease and one of the criteria is obesity, then you might choose *heart disease and obesity* as one key phrase. Using **keywords/phrases** will focus your search and yield the best results.

Part 1

Come up with 3-5 **keywords/phrases** for your topic that you pull from your criteria and do a keyword search using **three different search engines.** Save your most promising results in a file and label it: **KEYWORD FILE**. Find at least 5 results for each keyword/phrase. See my sample below:

Keyword/phrase #1: **Vampire Legends** (in this file I will list **3-5 articles** that discuss the vampire legend and make a citation for each);

(1) Hansen, C. (2005, November 11). Vampires in Colonial America. *Occult Journal, 68*(100), 42-47.; **In text citation:** (Hansen, 2005)

Keyword/phrase #2: **Vampires and Sensuality** (in this file I will list **3-5 articles** that discuss the sensual aspect of vampirism and make a citation for each)

(1) Janey, M. (2013, February 1). The Blood. *Vampire Journal*, *10*(23), 11-15.**In text citation**: (Janey, 2013)

(2) Brounstein, L. (2011). Why are vampires such a turn-on?.*Self*, *33*(12).**In text citation**: (Brounstein, 2011)

Keyword/phrase #3: Vampires and Fantasy (in this file I will **list 3-5 articles** that address man's desire for power over others and how vampires fill that need and make a citation for each);

(1) Rice, A. (2001, August 9). Interview by Jenna Barr [Web Based Recording]. The undead., Retrieved from http://youtube.com/ ; **In text citation** : (Rice, 2001)

Keyword/phrase #4: Vampires and Immortality (in this file I will list **3-5 articles** about man's desire to live forever and how the vampire satisfies that and make a citation for each)

(1) Bauer, B. (2009, January 25). Eternal life among the ruins. *Fantasy Times*, *46*(100), 25-30. Retrieved from http:/fantimes.net ; **In text citation: (Bauer, 2009)**

Part 2

For each of the above sources you found, you must create a **source card** and **in-text citation** which you will use later in your paper.

Here's how to do that:

- go to MS Word on your toolbar

- select the "Reference" tab

- go to: "Insert Citation"

- then click: "add new source"

Follow the directions and add the source material. This exercise accomplishes two things simultaneously: first, it records your source information for your bibliography; and second, it creates a citation for your source, which you can access later when you write your paper and add your in-text citations. Alternatively, you can also go to: http://www.citationmachine.net/*www.citationmachine.net*, make an electronic citation and save it in the appropriate file.

NOTE: After you complete this exercise, if you are not finding enough material on your topic, it will be necessary to go back and re-define your topic.

Once you have completed this exercise, you should have at least 15 sources for your paper.

Step 6: Taking notes

Taking notes from your sources will form the basis of the information you use to write a draft of your research paper. When taking notes you should use three methods: paraphrase, summary and quotations. (see Section III: How to avoid plagiarism)

Make a **Note Card** file in your computer. Use a note card(s) to take notes from *each* of your sources. Organize your note cards by your **Keywords/phrases.**

For example, my keyword/ phrases are: **vampires and legends, vampires and sensuality, vampires and immortality, vampires and fantasy.** Thus, I will take each keyword/phrase and find at least 3 sources and take notes on a separate notecard for each of my sources under each of my keyword/phrases which are located in my Keyword file. When I am finished, I should have at least 12-15 sources and corresponding notecards.

Here is a sample note card for one of my keyword/ phrases:

Keyword/Phrase: vampire legends
Note #1

Source: **Vampires Forever**

According to Mary Rice, The earliest vampire legends in America can be traced back to the early Virginia/ North Carolina settlements. In fact, there are legends that the Lost Colony of Roanoke Island was actually the victim of a vampire raid. "Messages carved in stones found buried in the surrounding woods seem to indicate a supernatural-type catastrophic event that precipitated the disappearance of the colony." (p.45)

And so on ... I will continue to paraphrase and use direct quotations from my article. Note that the page number is included for direct quotations.

As you record information on note cards, you should group your cards by keywords/phrases in the keyword file you established in Step 5. These keyword/phrase groups will correspond to the criteria you established in your thesis and become body paragraphs in your paper. Once you have finished taking all your notes, you are ready to read through the notes and write your research paper outline.

Step 7: Research Paper Outline

Writing an outline is an essential part of your paper. The outline, as stated earlier, is like your GPS. It focuses your paper and tells you exactly what direction your paper will take to arrive at the conclusion. As you go through the various steps in the research process, fill in the Research Outline Worksheet that follows. Once you have gone through the entire process, the worksheet will contain the information you will use to draft your paper.

These are the essential elements of a research outline:

Introduction (1-3 paragraphs)

- Provide background information to establish your topic, or trace its history

- Pose your focus question

- Write a thesis to establish the three-five criteria you will discuss in your paper to answer your focus question. *Each criteria should have at least 2-3 examples or case studies to support it. Each example should be at least one paragraph. The sample below contains 3 examples for each criteria, equaling 9 body paragraphs in total.*

Body Paragraphs:

1st Criteria

- Example, support (or case study) par 1

- Example, support (or case study) par 2

- Example, support (or case study) par 3

2nd Criteria

- Example, support (or case study) par 1

- Example, support (or case study) par 2

- Example, support (or case study) par 3

3rd Criteria

- Example, support (case study) par 1

- Example, support (case study) par 3

- Example, support (case study) par 3

Conclusion:

> Summarize all your criteria; restate the thesis; recommend a solution, add commentary (1 paragraph)

Once you have compiled an outline like the one above, it's easy to see how well organized your paper will be. After your outline is complete, writing the draft of your paper is practically done for you! You will have a chance to compose your own outline in Section II of this manual.

Step 8: Writing your draft

If you have followed Steps 1-7, you are now ready to compose your paper! Follow your outline and use your note cards to write your draft. Be sure to use paraphrase, summary and direct quotations blended with your own commentary. Download an MS Word research paper template from the File toolbar and type your paper directly onto the template. This will save you the job of having to format your paper manually. **(see Section III: Helpful Hints)**

However, if you prefer not to use the template, you can write your paper on a blank MS Word document.

When you have completed your draft, go to the next step.

Step 9: Inserting in-text citations, creating your cover and reference page

Part 1

Remember when you recorded all your source information when you filled out a bibliography card for each of your sources? You also created an in-text citation for each source at the same time. Now you need to place those citations at the appropriate places in your paper. To insert an in-text citation, go to the "Reference" tool and click on "Insert Citation." You will then see a list of all your citations from your sources. Position your cursor on your paper in the exact place you want the citation to appear, then click on the citation you want, and it will automatically appear in the place you designate:

When to Cite Sources

When you are:

- Using someone else's words exactly

- Using someone else's ideas or opinions

- Using unique expressions or wording of someone else

- Citing facts, statistics, images, tables

When Not to Cite Sources

When you are:

- Presenting a fact or idea commonly understood or accepted

- Presenting information that appears to have no author or source or is not the intellectual property of an individual

Part 2

After you have inserted your in-text citations, prepare your **cover page** using the **MS Word Template** you downloaded. If you do not want to use the template, simply go to a blank page.

Part 3

Once you have created your cover page, go to the end of your document template to the References page, place the cursor in the margin go to Bibliography on your References toolbar, and click "Insert bibliography." All of your sources will appear in alphabetical order. If you are not using the MS Word template, simply go to a blank page, type "References" in the center, and proceed as described above.

Like the in-text citations, your references were created each time you filled out a card for your source material. References should appear at the end of your paper on a separate page.

See sample below:

References

Anonymous. (2016, June 21). *Vampires*. Retrieved from Mythical Creatures: http://www.creatures/www.creatures of the night.com

Dunne, K. (2016, 1 22). *Mystics and Magic*. Retrieved from http://www.witches.org/www.witches.org.

Gregory, T. (2015, July 22). *I want to be a vampire*. Retrieved from http://www.scare.net/www.scare.net

Harrens, J. (2010). The Vampire Hero. *Journal of Fantasy Literature*, 18-21.

Mary Jones, K. S. (2017, January 10). *vampire lives*. Retrieved from the vampire journal: http://www.vampirejournal.org/

Rice, M. (2016). Vampires Forever. *Journal of Darkness*, 13-15.

Step 10: Revising/editing, finalizing and submitting your paper

When you are finished writing your paper, read over your draft, preferably aloud so you can *hear* any inconsistencies in language, sentence structure or general meaning. It is also advisable to give your research paper to someone else to get a "second pair of eyes" to review your work. Make any necessary changes at this point. Once you are happy with the content of your paper, use MS Word's spell and grammar check to proofread it. It's always a good idea to read your paper once more, just in case you want to make some last minute corrections. Once you are satisfied with your paper, take a deep breath and SUBMIT it to your instructor. If you have followed all of the steps in this guide, your paper will be a success!

Congratulations, you did it!

Your Turn

SECTION II – Your Turn!

Now it's time to put everything you've learned about easy research writing into action!

All you have to do is follow the samples provided in each step of Section I and fill in the blank worksheets in this section. Do not skip any of the steps listed in Section I. When you have completed this section, you will have all the information necessary to compose your research paper.

Step 1: Identifying Your Topic

Part 1

INTEREST INVENTORY

Select five (5) general topics that interest you and write them down, leaving enough space between each topic to *brainstorm*.

1. _____

_____

2. _____

_____

3. _____

_____

4. _____

_____

5. _____

_____

(if necessary, continue on a separate piece of paper.)

Now list everything that comes into your mind for each topic you wrote above. This is called **brainstorming.** When you are finished, look over each of your lists and highlight one subject in each list that interests you the most. Refer to sample in Section I.

Part 2

You should now have five (5) items of interest.

After you have finished, go over the items you highlighted and pick two (2) that are the most interesting to you. Write them below. These are now your **tentative research topics.**

Tentative research topics:

1. _____

_____

2. _____

_____

(if necessary, continue on a separate piece of paper.)

Part 3

Consider the potential of each of your tentative topics by doing a preliminary information search using at least two (2) of the following:

Consult an online encyclopedia like Encyclopedia Britannica, Scholarpedia (`http://www.scholarpedia.org/`), or consult `http://www.refdesk.com/` for a list of online encyclopedias. Additionally, you can consult the following:

- A specialized encyclopedia on your topic

- Google, Bing, Lycos, Yahoo

- The Virtual Library (`http://www.vlib.org/`)

- Google Scholar

- Infotrac/Proquest

Once you have found some articles (at least three on each topic), briefly skim through the material and decide which topic interests you the most and which one has the most information available. Write that topic below:

My research paper topic is:

1. _____

_____

This is now your **RESEARCH PAPER TOPIC** for all the activities that follow. If at any time you find this topic is not working out, **STOP** and go back to your interest inventory, select another topic and go through the same steps until you find a topic that you feel is workable.

Once you are satisfied with your topic, proceed to the next step.

Step 2: Narrowing your topic

Narrowing Your Topic Worksheet

Part 1

Write your topic down in the space below:

Topic:

Under the subheading: **Why I chose this topic** below, write all the reasons that influenced you to choose this topic.

Why I chose this topic:

(if necessary, continue on a separate piece of paper.)

Part 2

Next under the subheading: What I already know below, spend 5 minutes jotting down things you already know about your topic. (This can be facts, rumors, statistics, problems, controversies, misconceptions, observations—anything you know already)

What I already know:

_____

_____

_____

_____

_____

_____

_____

_____

_____

_____

_____

_____

(if necessary, continue on a separate piece of paper.)

Review your list and highlight the **one idea** that most interests you.

Part 3

Under the subheading **Questions** below, spend 15 minutes brainstorming a list of questions about the idea you highlighted above that you'd like to answer in your research. Make the list as long as possible.

Questions:

(if necessary, continue on a separate piece of paper.)

After you are finished, look over all your questions and *highlight* the one question that interests you the most. Refer to the sample in Section I

You are now ready to proceed to the next step.

Step 3: Formulating a focus question and research proposal

Focus Question Worksheet

Part 1

Go back to the question you selected at the end of Step 2.
This is your **focus question** and will form the basis of your paper.
Fill it in in the space below.

Focus Question:

_____

_____

_____

Part 2

Start another file and name it: **Additional Questions**.

Make a list of additional questions (at least five) relating to your focus question that you would like to answer in your research paper.

Additional Questions:

1. _____

_____

2. _____

_____

3.
_____

_____

4.
_____

_____

5.
_____

_____

_____

_____

(if necessary, continue on a separate piece of paper.)

Part 3

Next, decide what **the purpose** will be for your paper. Is it to *explore* your topic, to *argue* your point of view about your topic, or to *analyze* your topic?

- **To explore** – You are posing a question because you are not sure of the answer and wish to discover it in the process of your research.

- **To argue** – You have a very strong conviction or hunch about what the answer to your research question might be, and you want to affect your reader's thinking about it as well.

- **To analyze** – You begin with a theory about your question and then test it by collecting data, and then examining it and determining how closely it conforms to what you originally thought to be true.

Write your purpose in the space below

The purpose for my paper will be:

_____

_____

_____

Part 4

Next, you will need to come up with a *claim* or *theory* about your topic. The claim or theory is your position /understanding about your topic and what you will explore, argue or analyze in your paper. How do you come up with a claim/theory about your topic? Simply go over your Additional Questions list above and **highlight** the one that you would   like to discuss **in depth** in your paper. The answer to your question will be the **claim** or **theory** you are making about your topic. Copy it in the space below: (see sample in Section I)

My Claim/Theory is:

_____

_____

_____

Part 5

Formulate your **Research Proposal** using your focus question, your purpose, and your claim/theory in the space below (see sample in Section I):

Research Proposal:

Focus Question:

Purpose:

Claim/theory:

(if necessary, continue on a separate piece of paper.)

Now you are ready to begin your preliminary research.

Step 4: Formulating your thesis and establishing research criteria

Thesis Work Sheet:

Your thesis is a combination of your topic and your claim which you will then explore, argue or analyze according to 3-5 *criteria* that you establish. The best way to develop a thesis statement and establish criteria is to answer your focus question with 3-5 reasons (criteria), which can be drawn from your claim/theory.

Fill in the work sheet below. Refer to the sample in Section I, Step 4 as your guide.

Topic:
_____

_____

_____

Focus Question:
_____

_____

_____

Theory/claim:
_____

_____

_____

Using the above, formulate your thesis, breaking down your theory/claim into 3-5 points or criteria. Copy them below.

Thesis statement:

(criteria 1)

(criteria 2)

(criteria 3)

(criteria 4)

(criteria 5)

The criteria above will be used to find source material. Before proceeding, be sure to test your claim/theory for **logical fallacies** (see Section I: Step 4, Part 2). You are now ready to begin looking for your sources based on your criteria, which become the **keywords/phrases** you will use in your search.

Step 5: Identifying keywords/phrases

Part 1

Come up with 3-5 **keywords/phrases** for your topic that you pull from your criteria and do a keyword search using **three different search engines**. Find at least 5 results for each keyword/phrase and copy in the spaces below

KEYWORD/PHRASES FILE WORKSHEET

(Refer to Sample in Section I, Step 5 to fill out your worksheet)

Keyword/phrase #1

Sources:

1.

2.

3.

4.

5.

(if necessary, continue on a separate piece of paper.)

Keyword/phrase #2

Sources:

1.

2.

3.

4.

5.

(if necessary, continue on a separate piece of paper.)

Keyword/phrase #3

Sources:

1.

2.

3.

4.

5.

(if necessary, continue on a separate piece of paper.)

Keyword/phrase #4

Sources:

1.

2.

3.

4.

5.

(if necessary, continue on a separate piece of paper.)

Keyword/phrase #5

Sources:

1.

2.

3.

4.

5.

(if necessary, continue on a separate piece of paper.)

Part 2

For each of the above sources you found, you must create a **source card** and an **in-text citation** which you will use later in your paper.

Here's how to do that:

- go to MS Word on your toolbar

- select the "Reference" tab

- go to: "Insert Citation"

- then click: "add new source"

Follow the directions and add the source material. Alternatively, you can also go to: `http://www.citationmachine.net/`, make an electronic citation and save it in the appropriate file.

NOTE: After you complete this exercise, if you find you are not finding enough material on your topic, it will be necessary to go back and re-define your topic.

Once you have completed this exercise, you should have at least 15 sources for your paper.

Step 6: Taking notes

Make a **Note Card** file in your computer. Use a note card(s) to take notes from *each* of your sources. Organize your note cards by your **Keywords/phrases** (Refer to Sample note card in Step 6) When taking notes use **paraphrase, summary** and **direct quotations** (see Section III)

Use at least 3 sources for each keyword/phrase and take notes on a separate notecard for each one. When you are finished, you should have at least 12-15 sources and corresponding notecards.

Make a note card for each of your sources organized by keyword/phrases as follows:

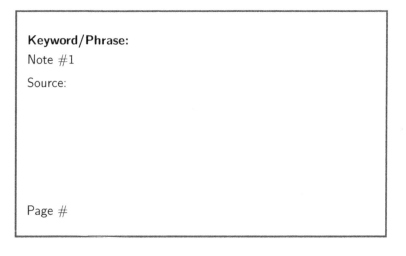

After you have recorded your information on note cards, remember to group your cards by keywords/phrases in your Keyword File. These keyword/phrase groups will correspond to the criteria you established in your thesis and become body paragraphs in your paper. Once you have finished taking all your notes, you are ready to read through the notes and write your research paper outline.

Step 7: Composing your outline

Use the following worksheet to compose your research paper outline using the information you have gathered in the preceding steps. (Refer to sample in Step 7)

RESEARCH OUTLINE WORKSHEET

Topic:

_____

_____

Introduction:

Background: (Give a short introduction to your topic)

_____

_____

Sources: (list any sources you used for the above)

_____

_____

Sources: (list any sources you used for the above)

_____

_____

Thesis: (copy your thesis which includes your claim and 3-5 reasons/criteria)

_____

_____

Body Paragraphs: (one paragraph for each support)

- **First Criteria:**

Support 1:

Sources:

Support 2:

Sources:

Support 3:

Sources:

Support 4:

Sources:

(if necessary, continue on a separate piece of paper.)

- **Second Criteria:**

Support 1:

Sources:

Support 2:

Sources:

Support 3:

Sources:

Support 4:

Sources:

(if necessary, continue on a separate piece of paper.)

- **Third Criteria:**

Support 1:

Sources:

Support 2:

Sources:

Support 3:

Sources:

Support 4:

Sources:

(if necessary, continue on a separate piece of paper.)

- **Fourth Criteria (if you have one)**

Support 1:

Sources:

Support 2:

Sources:

Support 3:

Sources:

Support 4:

Sources:

(if necessary, continue on a separate piece of paper.)

Conclusion: (sum up your paper by re-stating your thesis and offering closing remarks)

Sources:

_____

_____

_____

_____

_____

(if necessary, continue on a separate piece of paper.)

Step 8: Writing your draft

If you have followed Steps 1-7, you are now ready to compose your paper! Follow your outline and use your note cards to write the first draft. Be sure to use paraphrase, summary and direct quotations blended with your own commentary. Type your paper directly onto the **MS Word Template** you downloaded at the beginning of Step 1. If you prefer not to use the template, you can write your paper on a blank MS word document.

When you have completed your draft, go to the next step.

Step 9: Creating in-text citations, cover page, and reference page

Part 1

To insert an in-text citation, go to the "Reference" tool and click on "Insert Citation." You will then see a list of all your citations from your sources. Position your cursor on your paper in the exact place you want the citation to appear, then click on the citation you want, and it will automatically appear in the place you designate. (Refer to sample in Step 9 for the rest of this exercise)

When to Cite Sources
When you are:

- Using someone else's words exactly

- Using someone else's ideas or opinions

- Using unique expressions or wording of someone else

- Citing facts, statistics, images, tables

When Not to Cite Sources
When you are:

- Presenting a fact or idea commonly understood or accepted

- Presenting information that appears to have no author or source or is not the intellectual property of an individual

Part 2

After you have inserted your in-text citations, prepare your **cover page** using the **MS Word Template** you downloaded. If you do not want to use the template, simply go to a blank page.

Part 3

Once you have created your cover page, go to the end of the MS Word template to the References page, place the cursor in the margin, go to "Bibliography" on your References toolbar, and click "Insert bibliography." All of your sources will appear in alphabetical order. If you are not using the MS Word template, simply go to a blank page, type "References" in the center, and proceed as described above.

Like the in-text citations, your references were created each time you filled out a card for your source material. References should appear at the end of your paper on a separate page.

(Refer to sample in Step 9)

References

Step 10: Revising/editing, finalizing, submitting your paper

Read over your draft, preferably aloud so you can *hear* any inconsistencies in language, sentence structure or general meaning. It is also advisable to give your research paper to someone else to get a "second pair of eyes" to review your work. Make any necessary changes at this point. Once you are happy with the content of your paper, use MS Word's spell and grammar check to proofread it. It's always a good idea to read your paper once more, just in case you want to make some last minute corrections. Once you are satisfied with your paper, take a deep breath and SUBMIT it to your instructor. If you have followed all of the steps in this guide, your paper will be a success!

Helpful Hints

SECTION III — Helpful Hints

This section contains helpful *how-to* hints

- **How to use a template**

Using a template saves you the trouble of having to manually format your research paper. Before you begin writing the draft of your research paper, download the appropriate MS Word template.

Go to the **File** tool on your tool bar, click on **New** and type **research paper** into the search bar. A variety of choices will appear. Download either **APA** or **MLA** paper, depending on the style your college/university uses. Follow the instructions and write your paper directly on the template. Your template also contains cover and reference pages. You can delete sections that you are not using such as headers, footnotes, author notes, etc. How simple is that?!

Here is a sample (cover page only) APA style template downloaded from MS Word:

Running head

Add Title Here, up to 12 Words, on One to Two Lines
Author Name(s), First M. Last, Omit Titles and Degrees
Institutional Affiliation(s)

Author Note*

*If you do not want an author note, simply delete this

- **How to avoid plagiarism**

Plagiarism is presenting the work of others as your own and not giving credit to the original author. You can avoid plagiarism by using quotations, paraphrase, and summary in your paper and appropriately citing the source with an in-text citation. Student writers should use a combination of all three methods in research paper writing.

Remember:

Quotations must be identical to the original, using a narrow segment of the source. They must match the source document word for word and must be attributed to the original author.

Paraphrasing involves putting a section taken from source material into your own words. Paraphrases should differ from the original material in style and basic word choice while preserving the meaning and intent of the source. You must credit the original source with an in-text citation.

Summarizing involves putting the main idea(s) of source material into your own words, including only the main point(s). Summaries are substantially shorter than the original document and offer a general overview of the source material. Again, all summaries must be cited with an in-text citation.

Additional Support:

Here are some fun YouTube videos that illustrate the art of paraphrase and summary:

https://youtu.be/qoCdhJsS6Bw

https://youtu.be/EODtpSklitM

- **How to compose an abstract**

Next, you must write an abstract for your paper

What is an abstract?

An abstract is a concise summary of a research project or paper. It comes immediately AFTER your cover page. A well written abstract will make the reader want to learn more about your research, read your paper, or attend your presentation.

How long is an abstract?

Generally, abstracts are limited to one paragraph. Since it is the first thing your reader sees, your abstract should be brief (no more than 150 words for a short paper), informative, and above all, *interesting*. The abstract comes immediately AFTER your cover page.

TIP: An easy way to compose an abstract is to combine your topic, focus question, thesis and criteria into a single paragraph with a "killer" one sentence introduction that will "hook" your reader. Remember, the typical length for an abstract is about three-four sentences.

Sample abstract:

Title: Vampires Our Most Welcome Guests

Abstract

Throughout the centuries, literature has been intrigued by the vampire, from the hideous Nosferatu, to the black-hearted Count Dracula to the more modern version, *Twilight's* vampire jock, the handsome Edward Cullen. So why are we so drawn to vampires? Actually, it's hardly surprising that mankind has entertained an eternal fascination for the vampire because this mysterious **creature of legend appeals to our most basic instincts, allows us to engage in fantasy**, and ultimately **rewards us with immortality**.

Notice that what I did to create my abstract was to write a one sentence introduction, giving a little background information, then I followed with my focus question, answered it with my thesis and criteria (highlighted).

Notes

Notes

Notes

About the Author

J.C. Harold is an experienced editor and Instructor of Literature, English Composition, Research, Professional, and Creative Writing at several colleges and online. *Easy Research Writing* is the first manual/workbook in the **10 Simple Steps "Easy Writing"** series geared toward college students. J.C. Harold has also authored pet training manuals, dog breed books, TV series and fiction under various pseudonyms. Her latest series: *The Blood, Book 1: Secrets and Lies* by Brandylan James is currently available on Amazon Kindle. *Book 2: Awakening* is in progress.

Made in the USA
Monee, IL
28 February 2021